Let's Find Out About

Money

by Kathy Barabas

LET'S FIND OUT
BOOKS

Scholastic Inc.
New York   Toronto   London   Auckland   Sydney

We are grateful to the United States Mint for the opportunity to photograph
this book at the mint in Philadelphia, Pennsylvania.
Special thanks to Tim Grant and Mike White for their generous help.

Mint photographs by David Swanson
Cover photograph by David Vesey
Illustration by Ellen Joy Sasaki
Design by Alleycat Design, Inc.

Photographs: p. 3: Ken Biggs/Tony Stone Worldwide; p. 4: Hot Liquid, John Madere/The Stock Market;
Inset: Copper, A.W. Ambler/Photo Researchers. Inset: Nickel, M. et D. Bailleau/Photo Researchers;
p. 5: PMX Industries, Inc., Cedar Rapids, Iowa; pp. 10, 11: Coins, Ana Esperanza Nance;
p. 20: Bank, The Photo Works/Photo Researchers.

Library of Congress Cataloging-in-Publication Data
Barabas, Kathy, 1945-
    Let's find out about money / by Kathy Barabas; photographs by David Swanson.
        p. cm. — (Let's find out library)
    Summary: Text and photographs depict the process of making money, from ores to finished coins.
    ISBN 0-590-73803-8
    1. Money — Juvenile literature.   2. Coins — Juvenile literature.
    [1. Coins. 2. Money.] I. Title. II. Series.
    HG221.5.B29 1997
    332.4—dc21   96-44077
                                                                              CIP
                                                                              AC

Money!
Money!
Money!

Look at all these coins!
Where do they come from?
What are they made of?
How do the pictures get on them?

Let's find out!

nickel

copper

Coins really come from rocks.
The rocks contain copper or
nickel metal, which is melted
out in hot, hot furnaces.

The metal is pressed into strips and rolled onto giant spools.
Big trucks carry the strips to the United States Mint. That's our coin factory!

The mint has many machines that make coins.
This one, the blanking press, works like a cookie cutter!

The metal strip slides in.

Round blanks are punched out.

These blanks will be made into coins.
The scraps will be recycled.

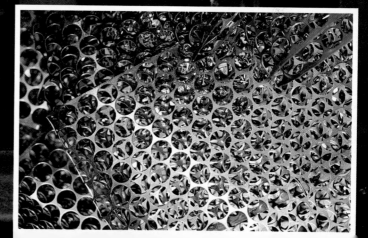

Bath time!
The metal blanks are washed and then tumbled dry.

Next, the riddling machine

shakes

out any mistakes...

...and the good blanks are ready to become coins!

What makes a coin a coin?

Words, numbers, and pictures change a blank into a coin.

Penny
Abraham Lincoln
16th President

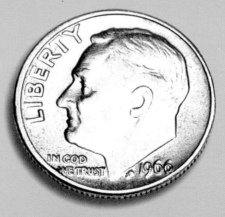

Dime
Franklin D. Roosevelt
32nd President

Nickel
Thomas Jefferson
3rd President

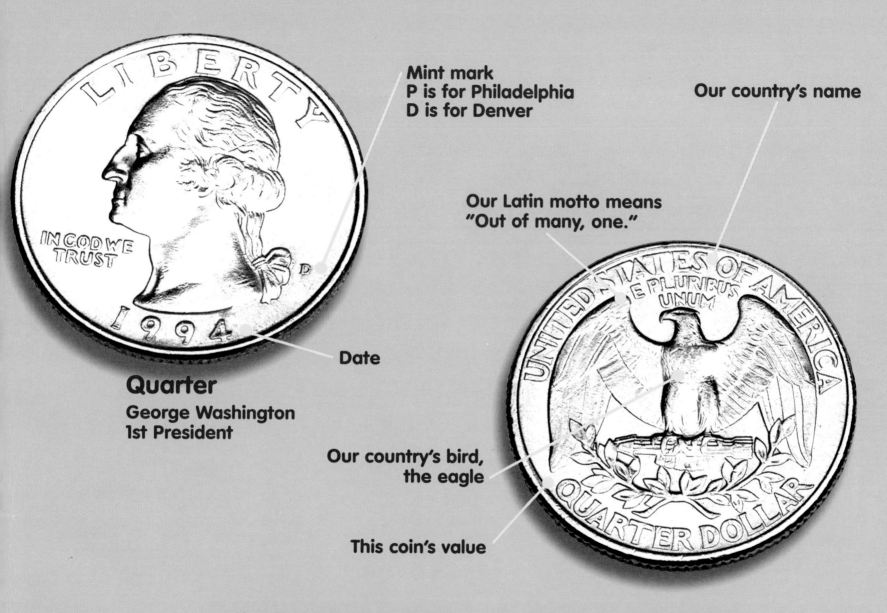

Mint mark
P is for Philadelphia
D is for Denver

Our country's name

Our Latin motto means
"Out of many, one."

Date

Quarter
George Washington
1st President

Our country's bird,
the eagle

This coin's value

Look closely! The designs on all these coins show
that this is the money of the United States.

Artists at the mint draw designs for each new coin.

Then they make
a **big** model
with all the words and pictures on it.

The big model is put on this engraving machine. It makes a smaller model called the hub.

It takes all day and
all night to make one hub.

hub

The hub is used to make a die. It takes over 150 tons of pressure to **push** the design down into the die.

blank die

hubbing press

blank die

hub

finished die

A die works like a rubber stamp.
It stamps the same design on thousands of coins.

Now this coin press turns blanks into coins. Two dies, a coin face and a coin back, stamp each coin.

Here come the coins,
hot off the press!
A worker checks them.
Next, the coins will be
counted and bagged.

Coins go
from the mint

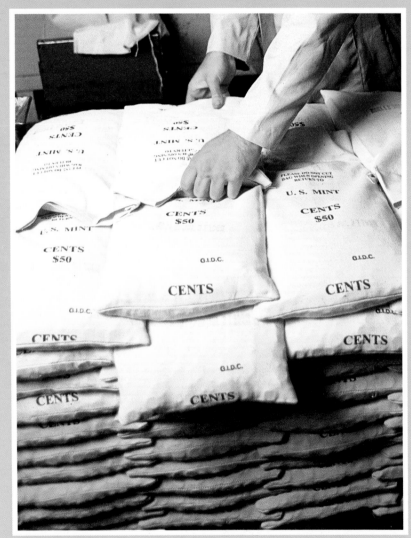

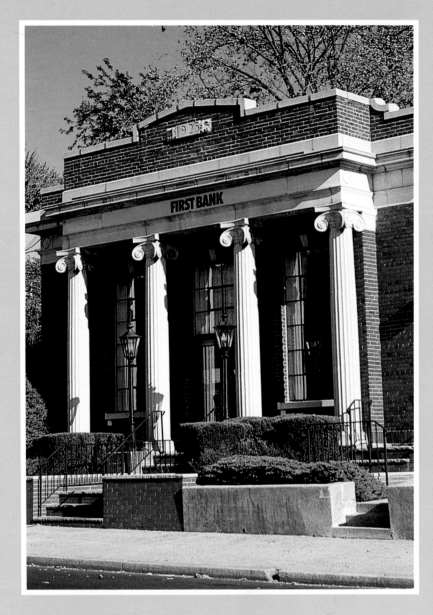

to the bank....

to you!

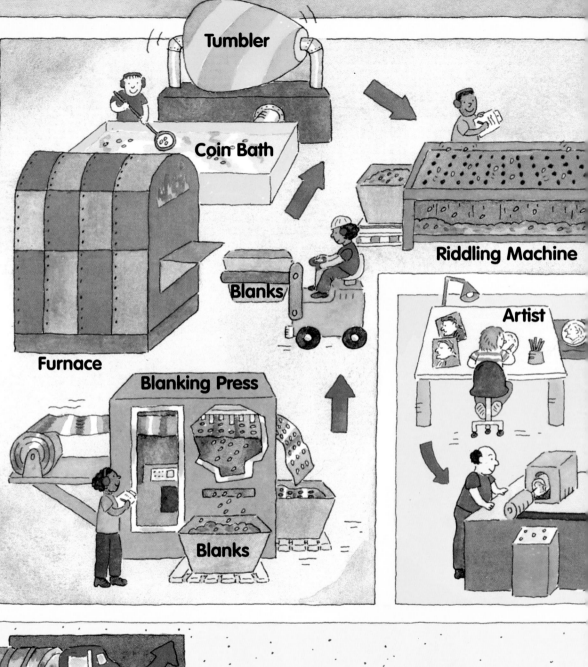

Mines

Blast Furnace

Rolling Mill

Metal Strips

Furnace

Blanks

Tumbler

Coin Bath

Riddling Machine

Blanking Press

Blanks

Artist

Dies

Coin Press

New Coins!

Upsetting Mill

BANK

Coin Models

Hubbing Press

New Dies

Counting

Engraving Machine

Bagging

U. S. MINT

Armored Car

ARMORED SERVICES

Things to Do

Before reading, find some coins to look at and ask, "What are they made of? What do you see on them? How do you think they are made?" Children may enjoy reviewing (and revising!) their guesses after reading.

Read and reread! Read once through the whole book. Then reread, taking time to look closely at each picture and talk about it.

Retell the sequence of coining. Use the illustration on pages 22–23 to help you tell the story.

Be the machines! Dramatize the sounds and actions of machines such as the blanking press, the riddling machine, the engraving machine, and the coin press.

Look closely at coins. Find out what year each one was minted. You can tell whether it was made in the mint at Denver or Philadelphia by looking for the mint mark, a *D* or a *P* on the face of the coin. Coins without a mint mark were also minted in Philadelphia, where this book was photographed!